Children's Room
MAIN

THE WORLD
OF NASCAR

THE BUSCH SERIES:
Shorter Races, Big Action

TRADITION BOOKS®
A New Tradition in Children's Publishing™
MAPLE PLAIN, MINNESOTA

BY TED BROCK

Published by **Tradition Books**® and distributed to the
school and library market by **The Child's World**®
P.O. Box 326
Chanhassen, MN 55317-0326
800/599-READ
http://www.childsworld.com

Photo Credits
Cover: Sports Gallery/Al Messerschmidt
AP/Wide World: 16, 17, 19, 25, 26
Corbis: 6, 7, 8
Dick Conway: 9, 10, 11, 13, 14
Sports Gallery: 5, 22, 23, 28 (Al Messerschmidt), 20 (Brian Spurlock)

An Editorial Directions book
Editorial Directions, Inc.: E. Russell Primm, Editorial Director; Katie Marsico and Elizabeth K.
Martin, Assistant Editors; Olivia Nellums, Editorial Assistant; Susan Hindman, Copy Editor;
Susan Ashley, Proofreader; Kevin Cunningham, Fact Checker; Tim Griffin/IndexServ, Indexer;
James Buckley Jr., Photo Researcher and Selector

The Design Lab: Kathy Petelinsek, Art Director and Designer; Kari Thornborough,
Page Production

Library of Congress Cataloging-in-Publication Data
Cataloging-in-Publication data for this title has been applied for and is available from the
United States Library of Congress.

Copyright © 2004 by Tradition Publishing Company, LLC

Printed in the United States of America.

**Note: Beginning with the 2004 season, the NASCAR
Winston Cup Series will be called the NASCAR Nextel
Cup Series.**

THE BUSCH SERIES

Table of Contents

INTRODUCTION

More than the Minors

Do you think of **NASCAR's Busch Grand National Series** as just "minor" league racing? Don't think it holds up against NASCAR's prestigious **Winston Cup Series?** Take a closer look at the Busch Series and see if you're maybe a little off course in your thinking.

Busch Series races aren't as long and grueling—or as well publicized—as Winston Cup races. Busch races are 100 to 200 miles (160 to 320 kilometers) shorter. Most Busch races are on Saturdays—appetizers for the hot-ticket Winston Cup feasts on Sundays. You won't see as many highlights or **Victory Lane** interviews of Busch Series drivers on TV either. And the roster of drivers is not as well known.

Busch Series cars are nearly the same as Winston Cup cars. Since 1986, Busch teams have been allowed to run current-year

cars, with shorter **wheelbases** than Winston Cup cars.

Speeds are a little slower because of engine restrictions.

But when it comes to all-out competition and racing thrills,

Busch Series events always match up. Bumper to bumper, door

to door, lap for lap—NASCAR excitement on Saturdays is every

bit as wild and dramatic as it is on Sundays.

NASCAR? Yep, but not Winston Cup. Joe Buford's
Busch Series car is covered with sponsors' logos,
but is not quite as powerful as a Winston Cup car.

The prize money and the **sponsorships** may not be as attractive as those of the Winston Cup. But there's something about Busch Series racing that can't be expressed in multi-million-dollar awards or sponsorship logos. There's more of an informal, down-home atmosphere. In short, the Busch Series might just be more fun than its bigger cousin. Since the series' beginnings in the 1950s, its drivers and fans have had one thing in common: They take their fun seriously.

Future Winston Cup star Matt Kenseth holds up the trophy he won at the Busch Series NAPA 300 race at Daytona in 2000.

C H A P T E R   O N E

Gas 'n' Go:
The Early Years

Racing pioneers did it the hard way. It took a little creativ-

ity and a lot of grit to win the overall championship in

the early decades of

NASCAR's Grand National

Series, which began in 1950.

Drivers scrambled to races

all over the country. The

best ones raced 60 to 90

times a year to earn points,

either in championship

races or so-called weekly

races at local tracks.

Stock car racing got its start on small tracks and in
beach races like this one in 1957 along Daytona Beach.

For most of the Grand National's first two decades, Late Model Sportsman stock cars raced alongside open-wheel Modifieds. Late Model Sportsman cars were pretty much the same as cars found driving on the streets. Modifieds had a variety of things done to them to make them into racers, such as bigger engines or slightly different bodies. In 1967, each got its own division. The Late Model Sportsman Series became the Busch Series in 1982.

The action was hard-hitting and high-speed in this 1965 Grand National race. The Grand National is the fore-runner of today's Busch Series.

Most of the time, Late Model Sportsman drivers raced in the very cars they'd driven to the track. Budgets were tight. Entry fees were often less than $100, and prize money was modest. Practically every **pit crew** member was a volunteer.

In 1981, the last year of Late Model Sportsman Series, driver Tommy Ellis won the overall championship. He went home with a sponsorship deal with Industrial Boiler for $20,000.

Top drivers such as Ellis, Jack Ingram, 1977 overall champion Butch Lindley, Bosco Lowe, Harry Gant, and L. D. Ottinger all had a shot at winning $2,000 or $3,000 a week—if they raced three or four times a week. Clearly, these guys were in it for more than the money.

Sam Ard (No. 00 car on right) was one of the Late Model Sportsman division top drivers throughout the 1960s and 1970s.

JACK INGRAM

Nobody knows the exact figure, but racing historians estimate Jack Ingram started more than 275 NASCAR Late Model Sportsman races. He won 31 of them, the second most of any driver. He also won a record five series championships, including two Busch Series titles.

History is clear, though, about the legend of Jack Ingram. If a **promoter** saw that a certain driver was dominating his track, he would call on Ingram. Ingram would roar into town and provide fans with a thrilling race every time. Ingram built his early reputation by beating future Winston Cup star Darrell Waltrip more than once in Nashville in the early 1970s.

From 1972 to 1974, Ingram won three straight Late Model Sportsman championships. But each of those years, Bill Dennis won the biggest event of the season, the opening race at Daytona International Speedway. Then in 1975, going into the final lap at Daytona, Ingram led a tight bunch that included Bill Dennis, Red Farmer, and Dennis Gireaux. Ingram dropped to fourth position on the backstretch. In a rush to the finish, Ingram came around the other cars on turn three for the first of his two career Daytona victories.

Jack Ingram won a record five season championships in the Late Model Sportsman division.

CHAPTER TWO

Busch Takes the Wheel

In 1982, Anheuser-Busch Company began sponsoring the series. It was known as the Budweiser Late Model Sportsman division until 1986, when it officially became the Busch Grand National Series.

Larry Pearson (No. 21) prepares to head out on the track for a 1986 race. Pearson was a two-time Busch Series champion.

Jack Ingram and Sam Ard dominated the first three years under the new sponsor. Ingram won the points championship in 1982 and 1985, and Ard took the title in 1983 and 1984. When Ard retired after the '84 season, Jimmy Hensley replaced him in the Thomas Bros. Country Ham No. 00 Oldsmobile. Hensley finished only 29 points behind Ingram in the 1985 championship.

Larry Pearson, the son of Winston Cup standout David Pearson, won consecutive Busch Series titles in 1986–87. He narrowly beat Brett Bodine that first year, but left runner-up Ingram well behind in '87. After the 1988 title went to another veteran, Tommy Ellis, it was time for a fresh face at the top.

In 1989, 20-year-old Rob Moroso outlasted Tommy Houston and Ellis to become the youngest points champion in Busch Series history.

Throughout the decade, the series grew in popularity; prize money slowly increased, too. Although races were shorter, the action was just as furious. The cars were slightly

smaller, but they were still reaching speeds nearing 150 miles

(241 km) per hour.

Busch Series action is just as hard-hitting and fender-bending as Winston Cup racing, as seen in this 1989 race.

It is hard to believe that Michael Waltrip survived the incredible crash that left his car looking like this, on the back of a flat bed truck.

The Busch Series' 1990 season included what many
believe to be the most frightening crash in NASCAR history.
On the 171st lap of a race in Bristol, Tennessee, on April 7,
1990, Michael Waltrip and Robert Pressley made contact com-
ing off turn two. Waltrip went into a guardrail, wiped it out,
and collided with the end of the backstretch wall.

Waltrip's car simply fell to pieces. Parts flew in every
direction as his wreck skidded down the track. Worried track
workers reached the scattered heap to save Waltrip. They
were about to use the Jaws of Life to extract him from the
wreckage, when he surprised them by talking them out of it.

Amazingly, Waltrip was unhurt. He crawled through a
small opening shaped by the roll bar that had saved his life.
An ambulance took him to a nearby hospital to get checked
out. He was released and actually raced the next day in
Bristol's Winston Cup event.

SHAWNA ROBINSON BREAKS NEW GROUND

Shawna Robinson developed her competitive skills in the 1980s and early 1990s, racing trucks and driving in the NASCAR Dash Series. In March 1994, Robinson became the first woman in NASCAR history to win the pole position in a Busch Series event. She qualified with a track-speed record of 174.33 miles (280 km) per hour at Atlanta Motor Speedway.

On the first lap of that race, Mike Wallace drove under Robinson on the third turn. She collided with Joe Nemechek. Robinson and Nemechek were out of the race.

Afterward, an angry Robinson told ESPN, "I'm working hard to get where I am. If somebody just can't take the fact that a woman's in racing, and he thinks he's gonna do something like that, I'm not walking away."

Robinson was true to her word. She stayed in Busch racing through 1995. In 1999, she returned to the track after four years away and kept breaking new ground for female drivers. In 2001, the mother of two made her first Winston Cup start in Michigan. She became the first woman since Janet Guthrie in 1980 to finish a Winston Cup race. Sponsored by BAM Racing, she drove her No. 49 Dodge in 24 of the Winston Cup's 36 events.

Shawna Robinson was a racing pioneer, one of only a few women who have had success in stock car racing.

CHAPTER THREE

Minor League,
Major Competition

T he Busch Series and its former self, the Late Model

Sportsman division, have been around now for more

than half a century. By the

early 1990s, this division—NASCAR's

second level—was a fixture in the

racing world. And with the names

on its championship trophy chang-

ing almost yearly, the series couldn't

help but draw more fans every sea-

son. In its first 21 years as the Busch

Series, NASCAR's "junior circuit"

produced 15 different champions.

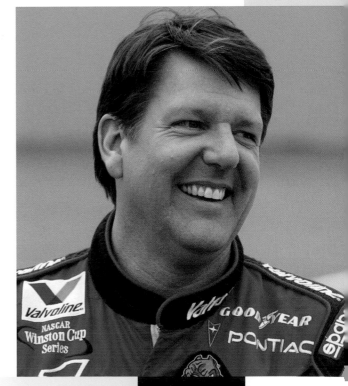

Johnny Benson was the 1995 champion after winning
rookie of the year honors in 1994. He drives in some
Winston Cup races today.

17

Rob Moroso, the circuit's bright new star in 1990, died in a nonracing auto accident that September. By then, Chuck Bown was on his way to winning the season points championship.

Terry Labonte, brother of Winston Cup star Bobby Labonte, defeated Kenny Wallace, brother of Winston Cup star Rusty Wallace, for the 1991 championship. Labonte again joined the title hunt in 1992, but Joe Nemechek narrowly edged him and Todd Bodine for the year's top spot.

Steve Grissom took advantage of David Green's engine problems to win the 1993 campaign, but Green came back to win in 1994, with Bobby Labonte as his car's owner.

Johnny Benson was Busch rookie of the year in 1994, then turned around and won the title in 1995. Veteran Randy LaJoie followed his narrow title victory over Green in 1996 with another championship in 1997. In winning the '97 title, he also became the first Busch driver with more than $1 million in winnings in one season.

Randy LaJoie won two Busch Series titles in a row and was the first driver to receive more than $1 million in annual winnings.

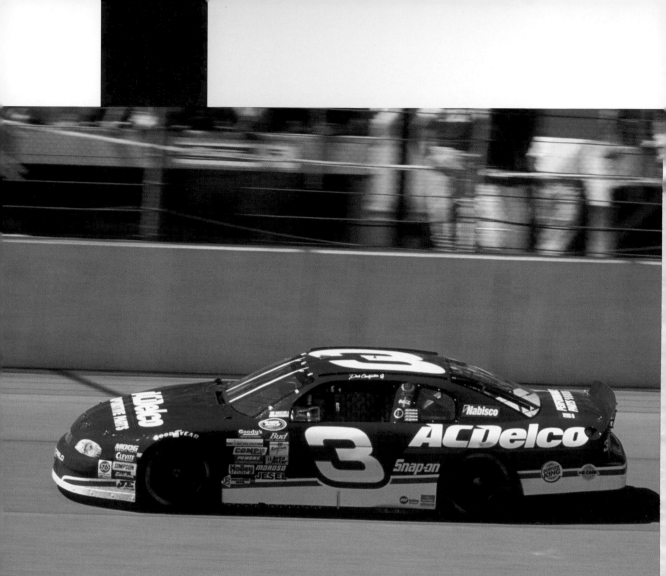

Dale Earnhardt Jr. won consecutive Busch titles in 1998–99. He held off Matt Kenseth in '98, and their rivalry drew attention to NASCAR's "junior" circuit. Both drivers, like others in recent years, graduated soon after to successful Winston Cup careers.

In a car bearing the No. 3 made famous by his father, Dale Earnhardt Jr. got his high-speed racing start in the Busch Series in 1998.

When Dale won his second straight points championship, it only enriched his family's Busch Series history. His father, the legendary Dale Earnhardt Sr., had been active in Busch racing. Between 1990 and 1994, the elder Earnhardt won five straight Busch races at Daytona International Speedway.

Earnhardt Jr. was on the brink of clinching the 1998 title after a second-place finish in Atlanta on November 7. It was a new feeling, to say the least. "I guess it will sink in," Earnhardt Jr. said, "once I see the look in my daddy's eyes next week."

By the time his 1999 Busch Series championship was secure, he spoke with authority. "When we won the championship in 1998, there wasn't a lot of pressure to win because we were rookies. So if we lost, that was our excuse. When you win a championship, people expect you to run like champions every year." Young Earnhardt used his Busch success as a springboard to becoming one of the top Winston Cup drivers.

Jeff Green reclaimed the Busch title in 2000 (winning almost $2 million) and was runner-up to Kevin Harvick in the 2001 standings. Greg Biffle got his first overall points victory in 2002 and took home more than $1 million. The "junior" circuit had come a long way from the days when drivers had to pay for their own gas!

Greg Biffle won the 2002 Busch Series championships, holding off several future Winston Cup stars to win.

GOIN' TRUCKIN'

In 1995, NASCAR debuted another national racing series. Instead of sending more cars out to the track, however, they started racing trucks. The Craftsman Truck Series drivers steer specially built pickup trucks around the same tracks that the Busch and Winston races use.

Trucks are less aerodynamic than cars, so in racing they can be harder to handle. But the boxy design makes it easier to **draft,** too, so the racing action is fast and tight. The sturdy trucks can "trade paint," as the drivers say, and keep racing.

Jack Sprague was a star of Craftsman racing, winning titles in 1997, 1999, and 2001. He also started every race from 1995 to 1999. Mike Bliss was the 2002 champion. Among the Winston Cup starters who have spent time in trucks are Kurt Busch, Mike Wallace, and Kevin Harvick. When Greg Biffle, the 2000 Craftsman champ, won the Busch Series in 2002, he became the only driver to win both Busch and Craftsman titles.

NASCAR trucks are high-tech racing machines. The backs are enclosed to help the truck cut through the air better.

CHAPTER FOUR

Graduating with Honor

NASCAR fans everywhere know the top names in Winston Cup racing. If they're students of NASCAR history, they also know that many of those elite drivers honed their skills at the wheel of Busch race cars.

There's a strong connection between NASCAR's top two levels. Busch events often are held on Saturdays at the same location as Sunday's Winston Cup events. So you'll often find Winston Cup drivers in Busch races. They go for prize money while also getting the feel of the track for the next day's longer competition.

Case in point: Winston Cup driver Jeff Burton won five of the 34 Busch races held in 2002, while the overall Busch points champion Greg Biffle won four.

Burton, with 20 career wins on the Busch circuit, isn't

the only Busch Series driver who also races on Sundays.

Others include all-time Busch race winner Mark Martin (45

victories). The late Dale Earnhardt won 23 Busch races and

Here's a familiar sight for racing fans: Mark Martin finishing out in front. Martin, also a big winner in Winston Cup, is the all-time Busch Series leader in wins.

In 2001, the year before he was one of Winston Cup's top rookies, Jimmie Johnson won this Busch Series race in Chicago.

two season championships before he became a Winston Cup legend.

Winston Cup stars such as Jeff Gordon, Dale Jarrett, Darrell and Michael Waltrip, and Terry and Bobby Labonte have appeared in Busch races. The Bodine brothers—Todd, Geoffrey, and Brett—have made Busch a family affair. They reached a total of 25 Busch victories when Todd won the Kroger 300 in June 2002.

Also in 2002, rookie star Jimmie Johnson used the skills he had learned in Busch racing to reach new heights for a first-year driver. Johnson, who finished fifth overall and won three Winston Cup races, credited Busch with teaching him to drive better. The races may be longer in Winston Cup, but the tight-driving, high-speed skills are the same.

And just like the major leagues in other sports, only the very best make the jump from Busch to Winston Cup. As you watch Busch races in the future, remember that you're watching the Winston Cup stars of tomorrow.

MARK MARTIN: WORKING WEEKENDS

Mark Martin is best known as a successful, veteran Winston Cup driver. But Martin has also spent a lot of time in Busch races. He holds the Busch Series record for the most victories—45. Only three of those wins came before he began driving at NASCAR's top level.

Martin is a perfect example of what makes the Busch Series so popular. He gave fans a chance to watch the best from both series go head to head on Saturday afternoons.

In Martin's Winston Cup career, he has 33 victories. He has also been runner-up for the season points championship four times—1990, 1994, 1998, and 2002.

Martin's first Busch victory came in 1987, his only full season on the "junior" tour. His best year in Busch was 1993, when he won seven of the 14 races he ran. Martin broke Jack Ingram's previous record of 31 victories in 1997. Almost all of those wins meant that Martin was driving up to 300 miles (480 km) on Saturdays and then up to 600 (960 km) more on Sundays!

"There have been years in my career when Busch racing was the only thing that brought me success," Martin said. However, he decided in 2000 to concentrate on the Winston Cup. "I will miss competing in the Busch Series. I have raced against some really good drivers, and it is an excellent source to find some of the upcoming stars of the sport."

Mark Martin is the best example of a driver using the skills he developed in Busch racing to achieve great success in Winston Cup.

THE BUSCH SERIES HISTORY

1950   NASCAR starts Grand National Series

1967   NASCAR Grand National Series splits into two divisions—Late Model Sportsman and Modified

1982   Anheuser-Busch begins its sponsorship, and the division's name changes to Budweiser Late Model Sportsman Series

1986   The division name changes to the Busch Grand National Series, as current-year cars with 105-inch wheelbases appear on the tour

1987   Mark Martin wins the first of his record 45 Busch Series races

1989   At age 20, Rob Moroso becomes the Busch Series' youngest points champion

1999   Dale Earnhardt Jr. wins his second consecutive Busch Series points championship, becoming the fourth driver to do so. Other repeat winners included Sam Ard (1983-84), Larry Pearson (1986–87), and Randy LaJoie (1996–97).

2000   Jeff Green posts 25 top-five finishes to win the Busch Series championship by 616 points, breaking two records held by Sam Ard for 16 years

2002   Greg Biffle becomes first driver to win Busch and Craftsman Truck series titles in a career

GLOSSARY

Busch Grand National Series—Since 1986, the official name of NASCAR's second-highest racing level, formerly known as Late Model Sportsman Series and Budweiser Late Model Sportsman Series (1982–86)

draft—the reduction of wind resistance that occurs when a car follows another car very closely, resulting in the back car using less energy

NASCAR—National Association for Stock Car Automobile Racing, the organizing group behind stock car racing

pit crew—the men and women who work on a race car during a race, in a special area on the infield of the track, doing jobs such as refueling and changing tires

promoter—a person who organizes and plans a race, gathering drivers and advertising to fans

sponsorships—money paid by companies to help race teams operate; in return, the teams promote the companies' products or services

Victory Lane—the area reserved for the winning driver and his team to celebrate and receive congratulations and awards after winning a race

wheelbase—the length of the car's axles

Winston Cup—the highest level of NASCAR stock car racing

FOR MORE INFORMATION ABOUT THE BUSCH SERIES

Books

Barber, Phil. *Dale Earnhardt: The Likeable Intimidator.* Excelsior, Minn.: Tradition Books, 2002.

Houston, Rick. *Second to None: The History of the NASCAR Busch Series.* Phoenix: David Bull Publishing, Inc., 2001.

Woods, Bob. *Dirt Track Daredevils: The History of NASCAR.* Excelsior, Minn.: Tradition Books, 2002.

Web Sites

Dale Earnhardt Jr.'s Site
http://www.dalejr.com
To learn about a former Busch Series champ now making it big in Winston Cup racing

ESPN
http://www.espn.com
For complete coverage of all NASCAR and Busch events

The Official Web Site of NASCAR
http://www.nascar.com
For an overview of each season of NASCAR, as well as the history of the sport, statistics, and a dictionary of racing terms

Sporting News: NASCAR
http://www.sportingnews.com
For more information about NASCAR from a leading provider of NASCAR information

INDEX

ABOUT THE AUTHOR

Ted Brock has been writing books and articles about sports since 1972. He was an editor and writer with the NFL, and has taught sports writing at the University of Southern California. He has contributed to the *Los Angeles Times* and *USA Weekend.* He helped produce Web sites for the 2000 Summer Olympics and 2002 Winter Olympics. Ted also wrote a book about great NASCAR families.